To the memory of my mother
Mary Dowling Daley
(1923-2010)

Contents

I

II

III

I

September

Hurricane shadow, then hurricane itself
skids across Long Island Sound.

Sodden leaves slap windowpanes.
They flail, then slump
under the scattershot rain.

Everyone home from school or work.
Everyone cleaning the attic of our old farmhouse,
my parents not yet begrudging each other
anything more perennial than passion or pain.

At attic east and attic west,
rain-smudged glass
in unpainted window frames
scrims the storm's brown and yellow glow.

Christmas gift wrap warps
where a leak misses
the aluminum pan. Outgrown
toys loom under roof beams
like an injunction against age
or betrayal. The box, cylindrical,
of Lincoln Logs—
remember how its notched pieces jibed
with the easy congruity
of man and woman's love?

This storm has assembled
what will diminish us.
It heaps, then pillages
our cast-off and windfall time.

My Mother Revisits the Scene of a Tryst with My Father at the Great Falls of the Potomac

There was the roar
of your skin, there
was your sweat
whistling itself upriver,
there were our goosebumped hairs
twining together
like squares in a net.

There was our rouse, our
eye-fastening-eye—
there where I dreamed you
perpetually salt-hot and shy.

I remember your girth,
the three quilts
you spread on the rocks
where we lay all afternoon
infesting the trillium
with our quarter-hour kisses
and our exultant sobs.

Far away and later, the speechless,
bleached contours of your jaw
that night we stalled
in the Parkway's maw.
We cracked to desolation then,
our edges nubbled
and milky as the windshield glass
glimmering in the breakdown lanes.

I still buckle
under the old taste
of your tongue's slow bruise;
still fret, marking your hand,
mute and sly,
where it once worked its furious glee.

I still listen for your torso
tuned square as a suitcase,
for the vows we soothed
with crossed fingers.

Here, in rapids
jostling a bilious remorse,
I drag back to your rampages
tricked out
as accomplice with scar.

My Mother Tells Me What She Was Thinking
While the Visiting Angel Gave Her a Bath

Then the lady Angel started spritzing
my thighs with the head
of a hand-held contraption.

Down there's where your father
lisped for a prize,
where he strutted

his bloated contingent.
And that's where you
headfirsters, blind and slick,

scraped your glossy scalps
and heaven knows why
you bristled and never looked

back. No longer muzzled
by your placentas,
your yelps slapped the pluck

from our love. When I fretted
too fiercely over
your browbeating hubbub,

your father cancelled both quiver
and shove. So I snubbed him
and his parish superstitions.

With every contraction
in every post-Eden birth,
I salute the smirk

in Eve's twinge. I bless
her broken water
and her trespassing teeth. Thanks

to her, we will all one day
fall—or swim—unbounded
by any womb

or a tub's clean porcelain,
forgetting
to drown or crawl.

My Mother Speaks to Patsy, Her Old Partner in Raucousness

Weren't we the two smoky dimples
of a barnburning smile?
Weren't we a buzz of each other's blenders

grating limeade sherry sours?
Life was a coffee can
gathering bacon fat to slick the rails

down which we flew,
oh, my rowdy Patsy!
Weren't the children

O-mouthed as they marveled over
our unruly upheavalings, our staple of one storm
to the other's windbreak?

Weren't we mutually utterly
dazed at the sayings
that would gawk

out of each other's mouth?
We starved our sadness with all
these high jinks, weirdly

chummy with the world
and so frequently bleak
when the world was without.

In an afterlife,
we'll be upbraided for mimicking
all the piousness elect,

and Patsy, you'll be docked
for mouthing the words
of the praise hymns all wrong.

Back on terra firma they will recite
the firestorm that was us, and how they rosied
in its afterburn. It's burning me yet,

the second and third degrees of it.

Prodigal at Point Reyes

The morning silvering, fish-tall,
foams over reefs.
Cramped with combustible oil,

dry eucalyptus leaves
brush a man's shoulders,
shuffle his griefs.

His throat brews new psalters;
heels trample small trails.
His nose gnaws the weather

of salt and bay laurel.
Sea wind creases his lips.
His neck, torqued to trouble,

twists where waves clap
quake-whittled cliffs.
Once kingpin of fibs,

he scrawled clues on his cuff.
Dull stars cured their shine
in the smoke of his bluff.

Derelict, dimeless, begrimed,
scion of a spendthrift house,
pulled down in perilous time.

Now dizzy, now doused
in blackberry ambrosia, in Armageddon
rumored from the opposite coast.

He might pitch, a pelican,
from stilled September flyways,
glut his beak in the lagoon

corralled by the switchback highway.
His world drifts
on fault lines grazing sideways.

Fables of terror and war lift
over paths where he trudges.
The sun shifts.

Silver fogs nudge
hills knotted brown.
Shark jaws, eager, flush,

flex at the round
of seals in their haul-outs
hounding herring down.

In a whalebone walkabout,
he unties the fire-blight of his smiles—
smiles scored like stone Buddhas, smiles that implode

snowing rock dust over pastures and shoals.
Miles mapping deceit,
chapped by tall tales.

Striding, drum-steady, he completes
the muster of his will. Once maimed,
now it stiffens and greets

all the new-minted truth he can claim,
prodigal as eucalyptus oil
verging on flame.

My Mother Explains My Father's Wanton and Serial Philandering

Some say I pushed him into it
with my bad broom
and my bungling sponge. Some say

I should have rebuked him
when he sweet-talked me back
to his lunge. Your father's calves

and knees built a ladder
I might climb
towards heaven—or a noose.

I was a girl accustomed to lavish;
your father was merely
profuse. Though he kept me

in wishbones and feathers,
my gizzard was starved of its grit.
If he promised a raft

of fine weathers, I nearly drowned
in rain splashed from his spit. I lived
for my head and he lived

for his *glans*. His training
was for a forever of Christmas
mornings. One finger laid aside

his nose, he began to fly up
new chimneys without warning. Dubbing me
"Miss Coal-Picking Sisyphus,

Purveyor to Stockings and Socks,"
he left me here mining pinpricks
of fossilized bliss from the veins

of my voodoo doll heart.

With Girl, Heading Towards Annisquam Light

When we kissed, you were consigning
some portion of your later years
to part-time spinster,
were offering the world
swagger in a white sweatshirt, were
asking the glory
of your Azorean legacies
to spell themselves out
in the code of a lit cigarette tip
circling in the starlight.
You kissed me on the way down
and my brother on the way up,
the lighthouse like a lipstick tube
screwed open to the chapped night,
the sand warm as new ash,
the blue evening shading into razor,
into something scratched
and scored beyond your smoke.

What My Mother Forgot to Tell
My Only Living Brother on His Birthday

Goodbye, my boy, Rooster,
whittling at your phantom perch
inside the barn the last tenant torched

before we came, spry and easy,
to that kind, prickly kingdom
of the raspberry cane.

Goodbye, mean thicket.
Goodbye, shuttered well. Goodbye,
you old gray tongue of tainted groundwater.

Son, we will you a tree house
to howl from or scan all creation—
boy in your chokehold colic, sporting

the jam-stained jersey of a denatured soul,
the blazon of not enough and not enough.
You wept us baffling

out of your live traps and trials,
your cruelties consumed
and revived. We recall your inaccurate pitch,

your sorrow and rough,
your conjuring strange without willing it,
your small fires in the rage,

your garbage cans too zinc to blaze,
your always smelling
of my sour breasts and tick repellent.

Discard your guitar picks,
son of my Rayon Age,
and tell me why moths

scorch their pioneer shapes
in the lining of your pockets,
why you clambered up the rainspout,

then drizzled from the gutter, then collected
your wrists into cherrybomb boasts, into
spikes in the spokes of far better.

My Mother Speaks with Two Police Officers
Who Arrive at Her Door on Good Friday Afternoon

What was his poison? Short days
getting longer. They were only old taunts,
but they soaped all his mirrors.

Gentlemen, come see our piano,
its black keys all stooped
by the weight of his knuckles.

Here's a hope chest
where mothballs
seal the rot in his slapstick.

They hoard the stains where his T-shirts
sweated out Trotskyist proverbs.
Here's a cruet for his chrism,

a vat for his vinegar.
See? That sticky flytrap
dangles his tear salts

with the smut from his incense.
These holes in his sock drawer
stung the hands of their darner.

*

You speak of a building roof,
of a leap so exotic—
(so unlike how he drowned

our garage in distemper)
—the last of his cigarettes
slammed for the heartbreak,

windburn and brownout
as he spilled through the downdrafts,
blown kiss for the boys

he had chased into whiplash.
Did he shake off his skin
or tear it to toothache?

Did my boy flatten his crown
or land on his hands?
On the tips of all that gravel,

split his shins into charms?

My Mother Contemplates the Decisions

A decay of tears, and then
their moldy trust.
I am a freight car

tilting off a shoulder.
I am rain ahead, drained
to realms of rust. Will they hand me

over to the sponge baths
and the shifts? They say, *Choose*
or flop. Your options come either

to scratch or scrutiny.
There is no comfort
to collect from such a thirsty history.

Would I could snooze under an abacus
of wool and hooves. Instead I huddle
in a slump with my cross-stitch

or clutch or puzzle. All night.
No praise trips
through muzzled dial tones

past my lips. I step or burp,
snarled on snake-oil's drip
or lied to by the cunning

and the contrived—
a woman sucker-switched
and swatting wide.

My Mother Calls Her Portfolio Manager
in the Middle of a Bad Week on the Market

Your rallies were shod by banana peel blacksmiths.
Yours is the Republic of Crash and Crying Out Loud.
Now you have nothing to lead us—
just a darker tint to your limousine windows
as you skitter off
to one more drive-by crisis.

What do you mean by subterranean economies?
If these dips are mavericks,
are they thirsty calves, then,
bleating for their brands?
I am wise to your feints, to your doping indicators,
to your tribe of tyro soothsayers who teethed
on their own sound bites.

Sir, I am proud
of my prudent weather. I never swore
off my sweeteners completely,
but I know how to stretch the dregs
in a bottle of ketchup. I cancelled the milkman
long before you cashed in your Krugerrands.

But, my man! This is slapdash, this is kidnapping!
This is all my collectibles cheek-to-cheek
with the ukuleles
in the pawnshop window.
This is a deadletter box destination
for a mail-order bride.
These are the decades of tinned pilchards
against which you said you had me inoculated.

Boy, you're a relief pitcher
brokering a bases-loaded
with ball after ball after ball.
You're a bank teller whose foot just happened to forget
where the stick-up alarm floor pedal
roosts on its springs
in a thieving week just like this one.

My Mother Explains Why She Threw Away
All My Dolls

The kickball pitcher in second grade
warned that your team captain
would see you canned

when, to my dismay,
he found you clutching,
in each hand, a rag doll

sprouting mopstring hair. So,
I stashed your darlings
in the magical cache

of Junkfill Hill and The Land
of Ash—gray rabbit,
that brown with Brahms-for-a-heart bear.

I know I pledged my word
they'd be bustling
at your headboard again soon.

But you were turning scabbard
from sword and all the elixirs
in my spoon mean to soothe

you away from that feverish maze
you still stagger towards
in your girlish haze, my boy

with your dowsing stick bent
in the wrongest ways.
I was the Erasing Angel

poxing your mitten-thumb
Andys and Raggedy Anns,
your orange-furred puppet foxes

and pimple-fleece lambs.
Son, if you cannot speak
to sorrow in the full skin

of a man,
I will not hedge tomorrow
just to lose it in your hands.

Merman After Electric Ladyland

i.

Mr. Hendrix ballyhoos a hubbub. He rounds
lapsed time over a bass line, detonates drum mutinies.
Maestro divvies Red Seas into sound.
Coo and cough flag their wings, easy

in the weather of his guitar. Sleet, cloudclap, madness—
all stratocast between major chords.
Contents of a fretted shaker strained over ice.
O, perfection of switching promises and rewards!

Notes skitter, decamp their oases
to a Jerusalem divided in blood.
Jimi's fingers trill the timing. He's aglow as
cat fur smoked on a sunlit car hood.

He's mink as a milk-fed mouse lolling in the granary.
He's gnawed by the possibility

that all will be hellish, all manner of things
a luciferous diablo.
O, hellbird swinging
like the moon over tidal bores! O, ghetto

elevators creaking in your sleep! O, breast
of Gazan mother drizzled with milk! Tugged,
confined, kept close to the vest
like an unexploded grenade.

He excavates thunder
from a kaleidoscope. A procession of birdcalls
undulates under jet engine wonder.
He papers a hornet in high-hat cells.

Will Maestro blow the amps? Can his wah-wah cork the clock?
Squash of bee noise. Moon dividing into sparks.

Okay, Dad, you listening? These bells are your freckles smashing
in time to a pulley as it dings a flagpole

A noise you told us was the sound of the bell of a pirate ship
shipwrecked underwater

Now you swim forever underwater with a porcelain doll cradled
in your arms like a coral chalice

Feedback, gently blown through the amps—it's your voice coded
in static from the old vacuum tube radio on the kitchen table

Before you sprouted a merman's tail, you straddled the roof,
paintbrush in hand, salt marshes stinking left, bay water
curling blue and hopeless to your right

A flapping noise—a hundred fireflies that you set free in the
theater loom hugely in Saturday shadows as they swim in
front of the projector

Reverb and whistle—the decay of your eardrums, last flickering
of the synapses along your auditory nerve the day we left
you alone in the icestorm, alone forever in the icestorms

Now hear this! Mr. Hendrix' voice is sullen, is the unctuous,
slightly cracked voice you in your taunting temperature
would turn on women who could not help themselves

Per your instructions at the drug store we help ourselves to
boxes of small fireballs yearning and plush in their
cellophane windows

Trace of Ohio now in Jimi's twang, trace of your friend Jake

The crash cymbals rattle Jake and his coy, gee-whillikers beer
breath and spotted teeth

There where you and he exchange maraschino cherries and sales
tips and phone numbers of easy women in Marietta

I sit on your double bed, the four posters shorn of swags and curtains, and you hold the handkerchief over my nose and you say, "Blow"

Both of us turned inside out to the sad torpedo misfires in our lives

Dad, this is metal hiss, a technical term. You never taught me anything technical, only how to sleep at inappropriate moments, snore at Sunday dinner

Also the importance of flossing the molars and maintenance of the foreskin

The snare and the rhythm guitar have been synchronized, and your bomber crew's watches have been synchronized

Your sweat comes up with smell of Philippines and antimalarial medicine that poisons you and makes you smear shit on the padded walls of the sanitarium

A flute in the corner—is that you in the corner? Your shadow Easter morning adjusting the menthol rub in the vaporizer when I lay croupy and wheezy, dreaming of green nylon grass and jelly bean wax?

Drum thud—you smooth my coverlet

Chir of flute and you stalk away underneath the South China Sea

Tape sizzle over headphones—your tail fins shoosh and shoosh, you curse and bless as best you can under all those far fathoms

II

My Mother Imagines She Is Speaking to My Father on the Twentieth Anniversary of Their Divorce

Dear traitor, when you tripped from sleep,
did dreams of me encumber you?
That day we drove all night to find
cold whitecaps shuffling into view;
short clouds that stamped and surged against
a bay that had abandoned blue;
stung sand the wind had wrung from grace.
In place of sun, a petrel gray;
in place of love, a latent truce;
in place of time, our new dismay.
So loved, you could not know the why
nor understand the strange complaint
I lodged against the lowering sky
that woke you up to this restraint.

My Mother's Instructions for How to Prepare
for a Last Phone Call with a Dying Ex-Husband

Find an uncomfortable chair.

There are old letters from a bomber pilot in the South Pacific.
   Discard them.

Do not conjure the lemony rot in the collar of his pajama top.

Find the ear syringe behind the ice cap in the medicine cabinet.

Give up vindictive nightmares for Lent.

Try on the dead dog's collar that hangs on a nail in the
   basement.

Pull all the brown leaves off the geraniums.

Apply hot compresses of clam broth to your forehead.

Research the pain indices for bone cancer generated by
   malignant tumors in the prostate.

Invite the children over to watch home movies, and when they
   arrive, take a long trip in the car.

Inquire about the current rates at the motel where you checked
   in the afternoon you found the tacky, sequined lady's
   cigarette case on the passenger side of the front seat of the
   Falcon station wagon.

Search scrap metal junkyards for the cast iron skillet you threw
   at him on Mother's Day, and missed.

Turn over the mattress.

My Mother's Utterances on the
Feast of Corpus Christi

Say what you will about superstition, my son,
these incantations always begin
from a clean low tide.
They begin in the glint of the gold paten,
in my dream in which the Eucharistic monstrance
is always stretching its spokes,
always etching the halo
surrounding its holy porthole
with the signatures
of recently banished saints.
They begin in that sleep
in which the body of Christ
is a perfect, papery coin
minted and pinched.

Back in the sacristy,
this has to mean something more than parish halls
plump with donuts and powdered creamer,
something more than frowning over skirt hems
and forehead ash, something more than polemics
on the problem of proper storage
of the unused Hosts.

Sadly, for you and your ilk,
the pastor has banished
the roller coaster from next year's parish fair.
The Lithuanian priest sounds wistful
when he calls to ask why you are not at practice
for your role as cantor
in Saturday's C.C.D. Mass.

After confession, dribbling their penance,
the penitents here
imagine but do not linger over
the wafer bits nesting
in the beards of the Apostles,
the holy water prisms trailing

the descent of the Holy Ghost,
the nine-month heaviness of the Virgin Mary.
O, Mary, mother beseeched
as collection envelopes
are licked and dropped,
then opened and salted in steep vaults!

My son, your brother
disappeared into the choir loft
and came back miming a suicide,
came back as Assisi, came back
as burlap sack petitioner,
wheezy and scratching,
with package twine for a belt.

Your older brother knelt
and quavered and sneered,
bowing at the tabernacle
with his native blemishes,
his cigarette pack in the pocket of his white shirt,
his star-ruled perturbations,
his canonical sadness, his drolleries
tucked under his altar boy cassock.

Was your sister too young to require a veil?
We don't remember her with a thing on her head.
We remember her tomboy knee,
the swag of her pixie bang,
her precocious tidiness, her diffident kindness,
her stifle under the heat lightning
of three braggart brothers,
her tunafish rash on Fridays.

Your father's hair has been oiled by ladies
whom even Jesus would recommend.
The ladies turn on the axis
of your father's yellow mouth.
They spin through his half-acre of freckles,
finger the hitch of his spandex pants.

He and the saints have this in common:
they were christened and moved from this to that.
They dipped their stamens, their sore fingers,
their blisters in the same font.
His sperm was an acid
cratering the urethane mattresses
he sampled and then sold
to grant us our monthly bread.

But now his prayerfulness has looped and crashed
and Blessed Sacrament parish has become the province
of the personnel department
of Central Intelligence, red-haired gentles
who smile without crookedness
and pass on recommendations
for new hires based on the way
the prospective molemaster crosses his legs
or blinks. When the percolator burbles
during prayer sessions in our living room,
you can taste their spooky effusions.

Civilian and spy, we
all bow our heads before the Nazarene's memoranda.
Our supplications seal themselves
into the rubber mounts of helicopter rotors,
rotors that rearrange the hair
of Army chaplains in their Mekong Delta clerical collars
delivering the body of Christ
to the medics and the scouts,
rotors that blister the water, that roil
our sanctified but unearned sleep,
that throb through the names we canonize
to fable our forever.

My Mother Imagines a Reunion of Her Children in California After Her Death

Fog, versatile and live, sprawling up the hillside, announcer and
  donor—

Fog, spill into the sun and save us from it.

There, by the lily pads spreading and spreading in the tarn
  where you—my family—are sleeping.

All your austerities convoked in microclimates of torn drop and
  basalt beaten to grain.

There you are, my old, childless children, who could neither care
  for nor carry the duties of perpetuity—

There you are with your record indolence, your pillow-proof
  apnea.

I hover and scrutinize; I tout, patrol; I issue my vaccinations.

It is to no avail. You are in the custody of an impulse grimy with
  extinction.

Fall, my stiff futures; fall, my sage smoke annulling the
  retribution of your blue fifties; fall, children—

There in your summer wondering over the polish on the poison
  oak which has overrun your sleep.

There you are climbing and firing down.

Speak, sickly sweet ones—speak, speak—of cloven hoof—deer
  or wild boar.

Show its hoofprint, colliding with the pattern of sandal, shoe, or
  boot—under needle and shadow, in glorious menthol,

In the minutes moistened by mediocre dribble, under leaf carpet
  and rout and the long code where dip met a cold,
  condensing doubt.

Where are the ponds you must cool with your useless lust?

Up over the edge of the mist the sun has warmed your
nakedness,

My dear disappointments, my flounders, my hurts who cannot
confound their own deficits—

At stake in bless and find—asleep in bobcat wail.

In a trough of non-potable water

Drained to boards the Redwood Age inscribed.

Here where mist hiccups the sun, sun that will remove your
jacket and hood—

Here you are in juniper grove, in spruce, in the red, dead
eucalyptus litter—the mickling water—

In a provision of sweet gravity, of the way molecules adhere—

Vaporizing in a gummy mugging of the sun.

Defiance

She is stepping backwards now
and laughing, the twin straps
of her bathing suit
looped over her upper arms.
The afternoon coppers
her hair; her rebuke
has softened like chalk.

The tide is yanking the wind
out to sea beyond her ears.
At her feet, the magma
has forsaken its fire.
All her life,
she has warded off caution
with her mouth.

It is not for nothing
that the world has left her so:
bare-legged, wanton,
bristling like a vapor trail
in the trap of the sun.

My Mother's Litany for the Feast Day of Saint Bibiana

O hangover saint scourged with whips tipped in lead,
patron of headaches, beckon the recalcitrant aide.
Ask her for powders to level my blood,
to muffle the shush of the thick and the dead,
to fatten these eyelids now peeled of their shade.
Confession is a tongue stroked into blare,
a sponge squeezing vinegar into each harried day.
My days fall ahead of themselves, then delay.
My flaccid hands bruise or scale, assaulted by stars.
Say that my mumbles suffice for your praise.
Say that my blank affect smells better than prayer,
that these tortures dissolve any heavenly bar,
that my bleeding brain bests your most glorious scar.

Before My Body

(after Susan Hester Breskman)

A short tree punctures the car window.
Bits of bark grasp the face
of the girl in the front seat. A blue voice
rustles a hungry innocence.

Out-of-range Julian, spattered with soup,
dribbles to a dry-lipped waiter.
The cloth of his suit is a small territory
where lost children sparkle like war medals.

Crisp as New Jersey, a widow eyes
a gray patch in sunlit sky. Next door,
next door, November—the wind
sways plastic bones in small circles.

Halloween hangs by its neck
over a tarp-covered pool.
Its beak beckons
the back-and-forth grass.

Julian, girl on his lap,
can feel the velvet shape
of her vagina shifting.
In a strange tongue,

the crash recites the girl.
Sunlight pierces the sound
of branches reaching for Julian's face.
It shields him like a war cry.

Prospect of My Mother on Moving Day

Her back coming up, curved and rolling, a hill-and-dale

Her back where the horizon falls off, where ships stalked away,
their mast tops like drills backing out of the sky

Her mouth where calcium slipped its grip, where nipple and
foreskin laid down their cariogenic larvae

Her mouth agape with the stammering consonants of rush hour

Her eyes with laser-stitched clear plastic discs, her irises milky
as coleslaw

Her chin whisked of wires

Her chin braced for trouble like a cornered gosling

Her lips shiny as boiled corn

Her cheeks darned by sunspots, her hair bleached white by the
northern lights

Her upper arms swaying like loose teeth

That space between her nose and lip flat as felt

Her nails notched like piano keys

Her eyelids twin lighthouses of apnea

Her nostrils in a singing stance, bent open for burnt rice

After a Stroke, My Mother Denounces a Nurse's Aide in the Rehab Clinic

The lady barb up a fire river
The lady yank at stitches
The lady dice fish with my fried
The lady scold to oversight
The lady set out portions and stab them
The lady brusque to Bejesus
When I do my eating with good fingers

The lady shifty and isotope
Her ghost towns thrashing yellowcake
Her reprimand Mass mushrooming on the radio

I am at sevens, collapsing
Germy
Weird to grated
Misstepped by million

She question my Africa postcard
The women in a row with one knee in the air
The women with their long dresses gripped in their hands
The women with a toe tracing a thrill in the dirt
The women with turbans
Or what do they call them there
The women grinning and griot, not for her
Not for her or for her

She wary my botching
My tattle sons and rattle daughter
My iceship and garter of frost
My parish of firehose baptisms
My mummers and my dry runs
My sprained bacon

Thaw the frisk
Thaw the hazard
Thaw the runny, the egg-poach

Thaw the fireweed
Thaw the derelict
Thaw the punch-up
Thaw the toasted thaw
Thaw the lady
The land in cleft hands
The belt of show and flinch

After a Stroke, My Mother Examines a Picture of the Icon of Our Lady of Guadalupe

Lady, why is your countenance
the color of vole feet
draggling from the jaws of a cat?
What tribe of mud daubers
stung stars onto your mantle?
Who names t'.e fumbles
that topple from your breasts?

Your counterspell blunts
the jagged crescent
of every campesino's
charmed and smoldering scythe.
Your spooled mouth waits to unfurl
the ticker tape of your vow.
In torchlight, your eyebrows
fly to heaven on thin wings of soot.
Only the moon survives
the crush of your heel.

Virgin of Guadalupe, I pray for your handshake,
I pray for your ribs, I pray for your hips,
the ones tugged dry
while expelling that bountiful head
ordained to gnaw
all the hangnails of history.

Steer me, Lady, through the lightning
that browns the mountains.
Drown the infections
that flush my cough into a gargle.
Virgin, who never burned a supper,
strip me of strangles, grizzles,
knots, of scratched jazz
skipping the shadows
out of my sleep.

Princess of the Aztecs,
thread my poncho with roses this winter
that I might adorn that tomb slab
where even cayenne would cool,
where your son's brain was looted
of its chemical salves,
and where his feet, which stretched the sea
smooth as a conga head,
refused to rest
at right angles to the ground.

Kiss me, mother of Mexico's hope—
your little mouth
is still rusty with smoke.

After a Stroke, My Mother Addresses the Lord in the Aftermath of the Earthquake in Haiti

Where are the women running, Lord,
their purses hooked on sleepless shoulders,
their streets flush with chairs,
with unshaven African gods?
Mason who made Port-au-Prince,
Mason who unmade the city in seven seconds,
you have made me, and ruined me.

Lord of cement and ricket,
you shaped us all in your own image—
every desiccated would-be grand-mère,
every lumpen soon-to-be amputee,
every mambo priestess consecrating her household altar
with a white candle and a glass of clear water.

Do I dare to say the morning sky
above this smashed *commune* is lovely,
the soft clouds smirched with a little pink?
It is your loveliness and it is everywhere—
Lord, your loveliness is in the scream and the triage,
in my own uncleanness, in my brain's perfidy.
Your loveliness is in the mash of wrists and shins,
in lean youths sturdying the beams
of their sniffer-frantic flashlights.

Your mother has emerged in the shape
of a wounded teenage girl.
Her scarred nostrils remember the flip flops
wrenched free from every
uptick on the Richter scale.
Her nose remembers the brio of my bed alarm,
my night sweats, my hospital johnny
ripping from chafe to chill.

Where are your disciples leading the Virgin, Lord,
one crooking Her right arm around his neck,
one gripping Her at Her underarm,
his fingers flailing epistles to the air
and tapping out the keen conundrum
of an omnipotent and merciful God?

My Mother's Litany for the Feast of the Presentation of the Blessed Virgin Mary

My girl has anointed me with cloves and pine,
with grapefruit, with essence of wingtip smoked
by flying too soon to Purgatory.
My irises are wet marbles, broken into lotteries.
Wild rice sprinkles the backs of my hands.
Head jammed against the pillow, my cheekbones
rise high as Geronimo's.
Meals scripted to soft mechanicals—one tooth,
three tooth—a bridge of sluggish dissolves.
Though my buttocks are loose and bruised,
when a cotton johnny slips my shoulder,
the skin there is young again, and clean as pewter.
White-nosed bats fixed to the roof of my mouth
itch themselves awake, and starve.

After a Stroke, and Infected by the
Bacterium Clostridium difficile, *My Mother Listens*
to the Morning News on Public Radio

For the Wichita pox and the measles
For the tuberculosis sanitarium, for the penitentiary
For the southern plains' slithering ice
For the tuberculars and their casino
For the pneumonia, sleeping out among the text messages
For the exposures in the felled rivers
For the slopes of styrofoam, for the exaggerated snowfall
For the visionary amputations, for the magi with their gangrene
For the mash of single digits
For the burning patriot in front of the gold-domed state house
And the New Year's without pumpkin soup

Bless the insurgency, the renunciations
The really bad guys versus the recapitulations
The fighters who are paid more than the farmers
The tribe or the sidelines
Bless the bypassing and the directly
Bless the coin, the worry, the women
Bless the advocates who cause the clock
Bless the spermy development, the opportunities
The decade troops, the sensible combat, the timeline of provide

I inhere and strategize
I mind neither sweetness nor phenomenon
I conflict with the walker women, the wheelchair sameness
I startle in the stubble where they topple
I expand with the dry diapers
I know they cannot know the gentle
I know they cannot blind recoveries
I know they are deciding my hydration
They are a hybrid and a wind chill
They are nearing their trances
That thing that happened to us
Their songs and despondencies
Their malfeasance, their dreadlocks, their tinted hair
Falling in a single braid to their waists

All interview long the cock's crow
Can single out the twenty-third psalm
The bishop has declared the earthquake the will of God
To build a new land out of beleaguered infections
To starve in the honor of the voodoo chiefs
Of the revolution's pact with the Devil
The hardest part is the living, the borders stacked like cordwood
The night wails, the dogs who list and keen
Always the staving off solid ground
The blunt of feed and house
The windowsill as projectile, the mattress as move forward.

After a Stroke, My Mother Imagines
She Is Bathsheba Thinking of King David

For my beloved is stout and wide.
His skin spills the smell of unblemished gold.
I hear his freckles
riffling and smearing.

Let his hipbones make a loud trample over mine.
Let his touch turn hot as a horse's flank.
Let my tongue shake the chlorine from his semen.

Even if his smile
has a bludgeon for a coda,
my nose will notch the gamut
from his ankle to the juncture
crossed by shaft and tuft.

Let his injury wrinkle my attention.
If my beloved is fickle,
still, I would douse his displeasure.
If my beloved is uneasy,
I quench his every noise.

After a Stroke, My Mother Examines a Photograph of Joe DiMaggio Seated with a Young Boy

There's still a gap between your hunger
and your hubris, still a coffee cup
in the right hand propped
between your legs' courtly spread eagle.
Your eyes are thinning to pin-striped slits;
the eyeballs under their lids
are twin fetuses at nine months
waiting to roll. I see, with a jolt,
the Arabs in Sicily. I see a man lathered
with none of his own expectation.
Joe, your hair wave is blacker than the shoals
of Isula dî Fimmini. It curls at me
like the mast-tips of a fishing fleet
sliding over the trough-and-climb
of an October storm, like a torn ligament
spilling from a jitney, like a death harder to reach
than the edge of an impossibly deep center
or deeper left field.

III

In Robert Thom's Painting,
The Governor Who Healed the Sick

*from a series of paintings entitled "The History of
Pharmacy" displayed in the window of Courts Drug Store,
Chapel Hill, North Carolina*

In Robert Thom's painting, *The Governor Who Healed the Sick,*
my mother appears, passive and Puritan,
holding the ladder back of a chair.
Behind her, a fireplace grunts and whistles,
empty in the bricked-up silence.
The governor, a huge man with a Robin Hood beard,
mixes orange liquids while
his apron skirts bend and shadow.
My mother wears the gaze of Delacroix's *Cleopatra—*
that is, she is looking away
from the business at hand
into the vacancy of the affair.
Her hands are unproportioned, grotesque.
Our old living room tries to emerge in this painting
in pewter plates that shock the surface.
The unfired wood in the fireplace is plasticine;
the pile seems to be glued together.
You can almost imagine
orange electric bulbs winking underneath it,
ruddying the silly room.
The angles of the room are ridiculously conceived—
the woodbox throws its lines
nowhere, the bedwarmer tilts
dizzily against the shelves.
My mother is composed;
there is none of that sadness that confounds you
when you see her tired picture in the scrapbook
with her eyes buried in melancholy.
The mouth is taut—
she has enough flesh to conceal
any teeth-clenching.

The open door, the clean fireplace
portend a warm season,
yet she is cloaked and capped.
Out of some sheer force of longing
she has slipped into this drama,
has conceded to wear stiff black boots
and watch a man, in her home,
administering to sickness.
She has accepted this irony;
you would expect some resistance.
However, a kind of stagy emptiness has seized her;
there is not even a flicker
of absurdity around her mouth.

Stone's Point

The fireflies split their sparks
over the bramble field behind the house,
fickle dots pricking the bushy dark.
On the ground, under tents of thorn and blade,
each female throbs, wife or killer,
each a pouch of damp light that flaunts,
then dims. Overhead, the male flies skim
small thermals—surfers crouching
over waves short but not yet torn.
They stammer, as if to say,
Gravity is a pact, not a bridle. Heaven
is the night we break our fire into fire again.
In the grass, peril is a pulse
that mimes the wanted thing.

After a Stroke, My Mother Listens
to a Chapter of Tolstoy's War and Peace

I think Easter egg broth,
nesting doll melanoma, moan
in the wagon rigging, the teeth of gears
blunted by sutlers and blandishers.

I am magnetite. I, the pole that corrodes the jaw.
I steer the terns winging through lice or arthritis.
I trust Russia, trust soldiers perishing for frost or camp char,
forage icicle, something to drink,
spontaneous shoe, stump out of blood.

Frostbite is an indifferent fever,
is a blackhead's Passion Play,
is a discharge of burning.

I wink in limp and sciatica,
the pain of forgiveness, the dull break
in dreams, splashing nicks
of a malnourished gratitude,
the trash of circumstance,
the old lady screaming in the outhouse,
the baby with its bonnet blistering
over stubbed-out cigar wounds.

I limn my humiliations, my pride drummed
into a cattle prod, my hideous tinnitus
splitting hairs in my inner ears,
malignant immortalities of zoo and hatchery.

I scrape at pestilence
and drafty fraternizations, at necrotized skin
scudding under gales, at legato, at slurs
and their hustler haunts, at rabies as strut,
rabies upbraided in spittoons.

I blink in repaired eyelids
strafed by the sun. My sucked thumb turns roar.
I think of my own cold cuneiform
after male truncations, of hunger
finding an old pot of stewed rooster,
of the sharp point of the badges.

Rocket In

Bodysurfing off the beach at West Gloucester,
our feet found your shoulders underwater.
Our hands snatched your hands
and we climbed your back
as if it were a missile pad—your hair matted down
as you crouched
in the teeth of high tide.

You lobbed us out to sea a hundred miles.
But the ripples we made ricocheted back
as bunching swells that teased
and bent the air so that far away
you could see them fatten,
coming in steady as comets—
a landscape of rows of molehills
shuddering over sandbars.

Minus your morphine drip and your catheter,
and with your freckled head itching with foam,
we imagine you here in this place as a boy—
phosphorescence blinking your skin,
clam noises and the smell
of the wind whirring through screens,
the spray of Sunday mornings dry and cool.

We sidle up to you
as you stand in the sand road.
Your eyes are careful. You squint at the sun.
You are wearing a sports jacket
and your red hair is licked back
with hair cream or the salt stiffness
of an early morning dip.

You must be on your way to Mass,
to eat the cardboard wafer
you believe is divine, Irish divine,
Irish Catholic in West Gloucester.

Now you are brawling in the back seat
with your sisters.
Now your father barks at the potholes
on the roller coaster road. You slip from the car,

sling into the waves with us.
We kick our way out
to the longest farthest sandbar. Way up the coast,
Mt. Agamenticus looms like a skellig,
the Isles of Shoals a Greek freighter in the blue haze.

The lighthouse beam angles you up
and out to sea a hundred miles.
It flares your skin into the sky.

Your freckles trail like ice
in the tails of comets now,
like phosphorescence in the bay foam.
They splay over the horizon,

shivered by storms when you rocket us in
on some bodysurfing West Gloucester day.

After a Stroke, My Mother Addresses Children in a Photograph of a Sidewalk in Port-au-Prince

The sign behind you reads *"École primaire."*
But if this is a primary school,
why are you schoolchildren

napping on the sidewalk, your sheets pulled
over your heads, your ankles dangling
over the curb? Someone has powdered

your legs. Someone has set you
on your backs to strain all morning
towards the pester and the shadow

behind the January sky. Children
of the *École primaire:* When we stricken
finally stand up and cross over

to the mouth of the shadow,
this is what we must say:
It is honorable to be stunned

and then revealed. Nothing
is mistaken but many things
are undermined. To heal is to betray

the grace that kindles every cataclysm.
Peace, children. If your last flinch
has thickened the frown

on the messenger puppet
who was nailed to the last
tree tilting at the last

of the cemetery wall, remember—
you were all felled by a concussion
louder and more terrible

than the trap door of the Tontons Macoutes.
The white dust that stifled
your breath whiffled itself

out of the hoofprints of an impatient
apocalypse. If we could see your faces,
they would be one spider scratch

of simper and wrench, one witness
vouching that under the crust
of the land, everything falls in fluid fire,

one testimony that the clumsy scattershot
of an empire's arbitrage is a colony
that shambles whenever the earth slips.

Patience, children. Forever will always
conjure something sweeter
than the back-alley odor of magic.

Patience—they will come for us
in their time—the dump truck
to lug us to the masked soldier,

the masked soldier to roll us
in white lime, the white lime
to peel our skin like paper off tin.

Though our tiny ear bones
spin like jacks in the aftershocks,
the coming cold rain will stir

every indignity out of our ashes.
The rain will clear our flimsy
copybook ciphers and letters

now blurred in dust
hoarded from cracks
in the shadows of hell.

Brokeback

Given your penchant for the goofy lampoon,
you might have dubbed it, "Poke-in-the-Sack Mountain."
Might have noted, with a smirk,
how in this film, the moon
is never anything but full

and always rolling
like a fluorescent communion wafer
between wheezing, prayerful clouds
rough-cut and tapered.

Your cringe would catch in your throat
if you could watch
that first spurt of roughneck sex,
bucked, as was your one and only shot,
off the back of a midnight debauch.

Brother, the shirts of these cowpokes
were bedraggled and worn
in the same weather
that touched off your terminal error:
believing a hidebound detachment
could be unraveled, then lured
to something more than a sometime tryst
in tender terror.

Their sex, like yours, never could meander
out of its parry-and-thrust.
Could never best, even in bitter candor,
obsession hunkered down
in rancorous, ham-handed lust.

Could never fall, with strange and simple fortune,
into a slaphappy, domestic funk.
The shirt on your back where you jumped,
when you smashed that charming punk

out of your head falling ten stories down,
was embroidered in yellow and brown
lassoed over a blood-thinned black
and more tattered than a cloud full of prayer
where gravity broke your back.

After a Stroke, My Mother Explains Purgatory

They say some burnt skins never recover
and skinned souls shed masks but never leave home
and fire is shyness, fire remembers
how far it fell from the kingdom of cold.
They say Purgatory, when we smell it,
spits like flickers along a fuse. I say
that Destiny is only the promise
of heat in mustard plaster's fierce degree.
Inside her shrine on a street in Gloucester,
the Lady of Good Voyage grips the man-
child who frowns down, as Precursor of Fire,
the cold schooner in his mother's right hand.
I bless the cool of the unlit tapers
there in her church. Do icebergs slice deeper

than any flame-wielding angel? There is
nothing more pure than the sweetness of cold.
Fireflies—souls Purgatory dismissed,
frost-green eyes that can't tear or twinge in smoke.
I say to live we collect things that burn.
Snow is the answer of heat-addled souls
to the scrawl of Purgatory's sirens—
sirens like sirens sprung by my oldest
whenever he pressed on that secret knot
on a tree in the woods behind our barn—
the slow sirens that notarize the heat
of volunteer firemen every noon.
Tonight, in a dry and cold December,
from the den's fat windows, I look over

at stiff firemen's hoses trained against
their own crowded patchwork of flame. There, they
practice in our field south of the rail fence
like grim altar boys with candle snuffers.
That's where, last summer, we sweltered and plucked,
plinked raspberries into buckets and cans.

Now, firemen's smoke shellacs shriveled relics
where they hang, gray as old dung, with their thorns.
Suddenly, my socks and shoes grow heavy.
I hear the burnt paws of field mice and shrews
tracking their black prints—random, unsteady,
flushed like fever from their holes and their lairs.
Now I know Purgatory will hobble
my charred soles through a fireman's rubble.

After a Stroke, My Mother Speaks to a Stuffed Pheasant in Her Son-in-Law's Living Room

Pheasant, I promised my sons
I will only leave them
to climb the hill to the long sleep

if you dare to fan your wings
in this room. Tell them my feet are
stirring in my black boots.

Tell them that my fists
have rubbed my eyes weary
keeping watch.

This room is cold, Pheasant.
Why do you roost here,
ruddy and betrayed?

In your indifferent pose,
your wing feathers are soft as Irish Setter hair,
your neck green as a pigeon's.

Your glass eye is weak.
You cannot take it out.
Do not let it cloud.

My dugs have failed, Pheasant.
They were nuzzle and buoy
and braver than cartilage.

Feather my breasts with your prayers, Pheasant,
for they have been hurt.
You have been hurt, too, Pheasant.

You were shot to please
a woman, and preserved.
Pheasant, it is wintry in my heart.

This winter starves me. The hill roads
near this house are crowned
with impassable ice.

Give me back my girl's ministrations.
Yes, her husband's backbone is maimed,
but let her attend to my squalor,

my blatant and durable envy.
If her man is courteous,
his pockets are bulging with buckshot.

His hands are forever tying tiny lures.
His hunt fills my girl's need.
He fishes her and fills her.

Pheasant, where will you fly to?
If I walk in your wake, will your turbulence warm me?
Even the fires in this house are futile.

Their smoke makes my sons cough.
Late at night I hear their gasping.
Pheasant, your cordovan coat

is splotched by their hacking.
They unlace my boots
and lie on the floor beside my bed

so that I will not follow you
and clamber to sleep
when you summon your wings.

Yes You May

for Deane Pless

She is the last mother now because
the earlier Mother-May-I mothers
have all been tagged
or fled indoors pimpled with mosquito
welts or just the hard luck of the dusk
that squirmed around opposite ends of the house
and flowed up the sloped lawn after these mothers
commanded tiny strides and pirouettes over
mint and crabgrass slicked
by mist the tidal river has pumped up the rocky bank
ever since the afternoon giant-stepped its way
over the peninsula where the last of the mothers
orders the entire flock to chase her
as she darts around the house
and when her own mother lunges to tag her
she the last mother
of that evening says *Turn around and look*
because the twilight has wedged itself
like a ragged rose placenta between
the hips of the hills that bracket the tide.

Half Moon Bay

Do you remember the pickup truck
with the cardboard sign
and tomato samples that silted our mouths
like the clay of a good Chianti?
Poached in the clashing heat
of packet salt and black pepper,
we skewered them
on plastic forks
and took them whole.

In the car,
under the breath
of a fourth Bloody Mary
poured from your thermos,
you said I was gray
as the mold that grows
on a greenhouse lime,
that I'd be fit to swallow
when I've skinned the shade
from my own shadow.

I forget sometimes
the exact flavor of your lip gloss,
how the fogbank that afternoon
dogged the coastal ridge,
the way you shove
a glove compartment shut.
But I remember those tomatoes—
how they plumped my throat
with their slurry and verve.

My Mother Speaks to Me
on the Morning of Her Cremation

When you remember me,
remember my eyes when you lifted
the lid off the cardboard box

for one last look. Remember
they were open, no coins to weight them
shut, gray-blue and fixed on the ceiling,

still and inert, taking in nothing,
beautiful in their purposelessness.
In the future I will come up in glimpses,

pieces of me looking around your corners,
fond and animated. But now my eyes
are resolute and unperturbed,

beyond stasis, ready for the fire,
in that place where damage
and healing are mutually suppressed,

where ambition and frustration
have steamed away between
the tiny ridges of a sand bar

leaving a little salt, a little grit.

Now Your Mother Is the Lord of Death

Now your mother is the Lord of Death.
Her ash is affluent and fugitive. She is where
tears spool their nylon line

over the sand where she combed and combed,
where she launched her messages to the gods
of cold salt and striped bass, the gods of drunken

fly fishermen, the gods face down
in the sand bar, gods like flies fixed in baby oil,
gods spooned into greenhead sandwiches.

I am the Lord of Death in small riptides, she says,
my forearms miming the girls from the Catholic camp
backstroking every day regardless of the weather,

shivering in their regulation white rubber caps.
I am the chapped sex in unsoundproofed
bedrooms partitioned by knotty pine.

I am the hands stained
with blueberry, dotted with butter, crimped
under the painted flour tins. I am the little smells

in the broom closet, the whiffs of old baby
trapped in decades of hot summer sun,
the attic where chilled children

warm their bones after all-day soaks
in salt water. I am water
so cold that ankles have forgotten shins.

Look at the jellyfish
like a capitol whose dome
has turned translucent,

the fish eggs like a bad wig, the fish eggs in their long
sheaf-like cases fringing the sand bars.
Remember the gull that bit the business

partner's girl. Smell the panic in the crotch,
she commands, the lecherous sideburns
fingering sleeping virgins

in the back seat of the car.
I am the morning after the Holy Cross reunion, she says,
setting out your plaid bathing suits on the beds,

the wind picking its ways between the dunes,
the quick, clean smell of dune grass
scribing hourglasses on the sand.

I am the flurries of chagrin shaved
into flakes by razor clams over old shipwrecks.
I am the half-burned

lobster shell in the incinerator ash
you must bury
every weekend

whether or not I am there
to remind you that to suffer
is to stand still.

Benediction

Braced between bric-a-brac on a bookshelf
sits the small framed snapshot
where your left eye slips
under the shine of the camera lens,
where your right eye smokes
like tailpipe exhaust.

You have wrestled a smile
out of an indolent glaze.
You are at the end of singing a note
you have held for a long time.

You stand in the back yard.
Lake-effect cloud cover blunts
the shingles on the houses. Beyond the roofs,
smokestacks and onion-dome churches
lacquer the sky with
incense and soot.

It is early November.
You are wearing a navy blue jersey
with three buttons.
Soon you will stun yourself
into the stupor of death.

Afternoon light honors and disturbs you.
Your smooth skin, your blue shirt have absorbed
their portion of the light.
What they shed is what I am given.

Bless with me now, brother,
the good ministration of the daylight
that swaddled you then
and still frames
an unmendable chaos of loss.

Self-Portrait Seated Beside My Mother's Corpse in the Memory Support Unit

My shoulders dip forward,
greased by a small sleep.
I've worried her brain's darkening zigzag
with my off-key prayer and my apostate lament.
Know it—my chorus of "Cockles and Mussels"
can't salve her soul as it lopes through the halls
lit by the white noise erupting
from the white noise machine.

I am explaining her late, uncharacteristic use
of the "n" word to her uncomplaining nurses.
As usual, I've wrecked what can be wrecked
with my petulant skepticism
even if that's not how I wanted to believe.
Too late! She's with her Nothing now.
She's with her Navajos, her Lithuanians,
her Brehon Law, her imaginary fund for rifles
for the hectoring nationalists
—a casual wish that made me cringe
under the crescendo of an Aretha complaint.

That's cousin Janice's message blinking green
whispers from the answering machine.
I should tell her cousin Janice is saying
how good she sounds on the old recording.
I should tell her this old world is steadying itself
for the splashdown of an asteroid,
the scurf of it snowing up another Ice Age.
I should tell her Lenin's mummy
gets disinfected weekly with a dose of quinine.

I should tell her—*Open your eyes—*
Here's your son who learned
to think "special" means "spurious,"
who misplaced his whimsy

when he would take a washcloth
to your fallen breasts after your stroke,
holding your shoulders as might a skating instructor
while you stood like a child
balancing on bicycle pedals,
a child who has never, not ever, abandoned her verve.

To Mima's Vase

Your
glaze
was
shaved
by lava.
Hieroglyphs
in cider dregs
cankered your lip.
Across your curves,
crows, slow as clay,
toss their toast-black
wings. Their color pools
like ladled mole light. You
burned that she might sing.
With heat leached from brush
fires, she hackled your neck.
She drizzled your back in ochre
clawed from the caves of Lascaux.
Somewhere in the scorched apple
of your earth, her hands still flame
like kiln fire.   Peel away your
singed papyrus husk and twine us
again in the wind and wheeling
of her grace.

Author's Note

The majority (but not all) of the poems in this collection are poems in the voice of a persona based on my mother and which are titled "My Mother Speaks," "My Mother Addresses," "My Mother Denounces," or the like.

Any persona poem is a kind of talking back, a switching of the mouthpiece we place over our own delicious and terrifying impulses at civilization's behest for the controlled scream of another. This act can be an act of permissiveness, even of licentiousness—we can say, on behalf of someone else, "[W]hat the most extravagant might possibly think without saying," as Thomas Wentworth Higginson characterized the very forthright Emily Dickinson in their first encounter. The nasty, curmudgeonly, hateful stance of the monk-narrator towards the prissy gardener-monk with whom he shares a table in Robert Browning's "Soliloquy of the Spanish Cloister" may have nothing to do with Robert Browning's personality or character, but Browning certainly had the imagination to reach for the vehemence of forbidden impulses and give them a kind of temporary lease in that poem.

Writing these poems in the voice of my mother enabled me to talk back, not just to her (and certainly some of this group of poems do that), but to have her persona give vent to my own grievances, wishes, and disappointments, and to my idea of what her grievances, wishes, and disappointments might have been. But the poems are not a mere fusion of my impulses and my idea of her character. The voice is an invention, one neither she nor I would entirely recognize. It is a voice suffused with an archness that my mother could adopt when it served her, but which she generally eschewed; with a vocabulary that she would have understood but rarely used; and with an agenda she wouldn't necessarily have consciously endorsed. The tone is the tone poetic license permits. The stance is a fiction that finds its facts in the bit of unbridling of the unconscious which writing often provokes.

My mother suffered, but bore her suffering largely in silence. In these poems, her persona gives expression to its anger and sadness but takes no responsibility for its own complicity. Revenge is rarely equitable.

Acknowledgments

Grateful acknowledgment is made to the editors and staff of the following journals in which poems from this collection have appeared, some in a slightly different form:

24Pearl: The Magazine: "Stone's Point"

30/30 Journal: "My Mother Calls Her Portfolio Manager in the Middle of a Bad Week on the Market," "My Mother Explains My Father's Wanton and Serial Philandering"

Arch: "After a Stroke, My Mother Denounces a Nurse's Aide in the Rehab Clinic"

Archipelago: "Defiance," "Merman After Electric Ladyland"

Asheville Poetry Review: "Before My Body"

Barrow Street: "Yes You May"

Briar Cliff Review: "My Mother Revisits the Scene of a Tryst with My Father at the Great Falls of the Potomac"

Cellar Door: "In Robert Thom's Painting, *The Governor Who Healed the Sick*"

Conte: "Now Your Mother Is the Lord of Death"

Denver Quarterly: "My Mother Contemplates the Decisions"

Existere: "With Girl, Heading Towards Annisquam Light"

Fence: "My Mother Speaks with Two Police Officers Who Arrive at Her Door on Good Friday Afternoon"

Harvard Review: "My Mother on Moving Day"

Hermeneutic Chaos: "My Mother Imagines a Reunion of Her Children in California After Her Death"

The Journal of Pedagogy, Pluralism, and Practice: "My Mother Explains Why She Threw Away All My Dolls," "What My Mother Forgot to Tell My Only Living Brother on His Birthday"

Massachusetts Review: "After a Stroke, My Mother Imagines She Is Bathsheba Thinking of King David"

the museum of americana: "After a Stroke, My Mother Examines a Photograph of Joe DiMaggio Seated with a Young Boy"

Poemeleon: "My Mother Speaks to Me on the Morning of Her Cremation"

Poetry Ireland Review: "Benediction"

Poets for Haiti Anthology: "After a Stroke, My Mother Addresses Children in a Photograph of a Sidewalk in Port-au-Prince"

Rhino: "After a Stroke, My Mother Examines a Picture of
the Icon of Our Lady of Guadalupe"
Southern Humanities Review: "Half Moon Bay"
Studio Potter: "To Mima's Vase"
The Café Review: "After a Stroke, My Mother Speaks to a
Stuffed Pheasant in her Son-in-Law's Living Room"
unsplendid: "Prodigal at Point Reyes"
Witness: "After a Stroke, My Mother Addresses the Lord
in the Aftermath of the Earthquake in Haiti," "My Mother
Listens to a Chapter of Tolstoy's *War and Peace*"

The following poems were also anthologized: "My Mother Calls
Her Portfolio Manager in the Middle of a Bad Week on the
Market" (*20 Years of the Cantab*) and "My Mother Revisits the
Scene of a Tryst with My Father at the Great Falls of the Potomac"
(*The Body Electric*). "Benediction," "Defiance," "Merman After
Electric Ladyland," "To Mima's Vase," and "In Robert Thom's
Painting, *The Governor Who Healed the Sick*" appeared in the
chapbook *Canticles and Inventories* (Wyngaerts Hoeck Press).

"My Mother Revisits the Scene of a Tryst with My Father at the
Great Falls of the Potomac," "My Mother Tells Me What She Was
Thinking While the Visiting Angel Gave Her a Bath," "My Mother's
Instructions for How to Prepare for a Last Phone Call with a Dying
Ex-Husband," "My Mother Explains Purgatory," and "Self-Portrait
Seated Beside My Mother's Corpse in the Memory Support Unit"
were awarded the 2012 Dana Award in Poetry.

"In Robert Thom's Painting, *The Governor Who Healed the Sick*"
won the Charles and Fanny Fay Wood Academy of American
Poets Prize.

I am grateful for the careful attention paid to some of these poems
in workshops led by Suzanne E. Berger (Lesley University); Lucie
Brock-Broido; Ethan Gilsdorf (Grub Street); Ellen Doré Watson and
Martha Rhodes (Colrain Poetry Manuscript Conference); and Bruce
Weigl (William Joiner Institute, UMass Boston); by participants
in the "Sunday in Brookline" workshop (Jen Kohl, Robin Linn,
Jessica Purdy, and Michelle Ryan); and by contributors to the
30/30 blog organized by Nicole Terez Dutton, where many of
these poems began to take shape.

Special thanks for support to this project by John Altobello, Simone Beaubien and the Boston Poetry Slam at the Cantab Lounge, Douglas Bishop, Daniel Bosch, Michael Brown and Valerie Lawson, Nicolai Cauchy, Mary Collins, Dorothy Derifield, Nicole Terez Dutton, Harris Gardner, Len Germinara and Sarah Oktay, Michael F. Gill, Ron and Sue Goba, Caitlin Grant, Philip Hasouris, Doug Holder, Joan Houlihan, Amy Jenness, Joan Kimball, Diane Kistner, Valerie Loveland, Tim Mannle, Fred Marchant, Gloria Mindock, Isabella Nebel, April Ossmann, Chad Parenteau, Mary Elizabeth Parker, Cheryl Perrault, Jeff Robinson, Lloyd Schwartz, Licia Sky, Sandee Storey, Dan Tobin, Sheila Twyman, Molly Lynn Watt, Afaa Michael Weaver, and Bruce Weigl.

Cover image from a circa-1941 studio photograph of the author's mother, Mary Dowling Daley (photographer unknown); background texture by Brenda Starr; author photo by Devin Altobello; cover and interior book design by Diane Kistner; ITC Garamond text and titling

About FutureCycle Press

FutureCycle Press is dedicated to publishing lasting English-language poetry books, chapbooks, and anthologies in both print-on-demand and ebook formats. Founded in 2007 by long-time independent editor/publishers and partners Diane Kistner and Robert S. King, the press incorporated as a nonprofit in 2012. A number of our editors are distinguished poets and writers in their own right, and we have been actively involved in the small press movement going back to the early seventies.

The FutureCycle Poetry Book Prize and honorarium is awarded annually for the best full-length volume of poetry we publish in a calendar year. Introduced in 2013, our Good Works projects are anthologies devoted to issues of universal significance, with all proceeds donated to a related worthy cause. Our Selected Poems series highlights contemporary poets with a substantial body of work to their credit; with this series we strive to resurrect work that has had limited distribution and is now out of print.

We are dedicated to giving all of the authors we publish the care their work deserves, making our catalog of titles the most diverse and distinguished it can be, and paying forward any earnings to fund more great books.

We've learned a few things about independent publishing over the years. We've also evolved a unique, resilient publishing model that allows us to focus mainly on vetting and preserving for posterity the most books of exceptional quality without becoming overwhelmed with bookkeeping and mailing, fundraising activities, or taxing editorial and production "bubbles." To find out more, come see us at www.futurecycle.org.

The FutureCycle Poetry Book Prize

All full-length volumes of poetry published by FutureCycle Press in a given calendar year are considered for the annual FutureCycle Poetry Book Prize. This allows us to consider each submission on its own merits, outside of the context of a contest. Too, the judges see the finished book, which will have benefitted from the beautiful book design and strong editorial gloss we're famous for.

The book ranked the best in judging is announced as the prize-winner in the subsequent year. There is no fixed monetary award; instead, the winning poet receives an honorarium of 20% of the total net royalties from all poetry books and chapbooks the press sold online in the year the winning book was published. The winner is also accorded the honor of being on the panel of judges for the next year's competition; all judges receive copies of all contending books to keep for their personal library.

Made in the USA
Charleston, SC
24 September 2015